A Step By Step Guide to a Clean Room

Clean Room

Table of Contents

Introduction...4

Chapter 1: Why is it hard to Maintain a Room...5

Cleaning is Hard Work 5

High Maintenance 6

Chapter 2: Overcoming the Problems....8

Mindset 8

Practice Cleaning 8

Tools...9

Changing Rags...10

Patience..11

Rewards 12

Chapter 3: How to minimize Tasks.....13

One Item a Day..13

Defense...14

Being Smart About Purchases 15

Decisiveness..15

Discipline 16

Reflection 17

Chapter 4: Minimizing Tasks......18

Focus..18

More Time...19

Less Pressure..20

Smarter Purchases 21

Stress Reduction 22

More Money 23

A Sense of Fulfillment 24

Chapter 5: Cleaning Your Room...26

Dealing with Clothes 26

The Big Picture 27

Laundry Hampers 27

The Monsters Under Your Bed 28

Making You Own Bed 29

Other Trash 30

Dressers 31

Declutter Your Room 32

Vacuuming Your Floor 33

Fresh Air 34

Conclusion.......35

Introduction

I want to thank you and congratulate you for purchasing the book "A Step By Step Guide to a Clean Room"

Another insurgency is occurring right now, one that looks set to change how we see ourselves and the items around us. This new, noteworthy transformation is the act of moderation.

Cleaning and sorting out your home can be a staggering undertaking because of overabundance jumble. This is particularly valid on the off chance that you are not rehearsing moderation. This book hopes to help you clean your home and show you about moderate association all the while.

This book contains various tips, systems, and techniques to help you clean your home and keep it that way unequivocally. We will experience every room of your home and supplying you with attempted and tried moderate hierarchical techniques.

Every one of these methods are separated into a simple to read with accommodating tips along the way.

Chapter 1: Why is it hard to Maintain a Room

Before we begin to teach you how to clean your house as quickly as possible, we want to begin by explaining why people fail to clean and keep an organized household. Identifying these two main problems will allow you to change your habits if you find yourself in one of these categories. They will also allow you to avoid these habits once you become aware of them. Avoiding large clean-up jobs and staying organized is all about having and practicing good habits. If you can eliminate the bad habits and pick up good, organizational ones, you will save time and money and keep yourself stress-free.

Cleaning is Hard Work

Many people have homes that appear clean and organized. Their counters are clean, floors swept, and bathrooms spotless. But under closer inspection, these homes are very disorganized and cluttered.

Closets are full of useless items, refrigerators are full of expired foods, and pantries are filled with broken items. Glancing in from the outside, these homes appear clean, but a closer look reveals another story. This is the current state of many homes today.

So why do most individuals never attempt to properly organize? Going through all those nooks and crannies, throwing out old items, and organizing everything in their homes is a gigantic undertaking. Just the thought of starting this process causes anxiety in most people. Who wants to spend an entire weekend organizing items that are not visible to most guests?

High Maintenance

The second problem that most people suffer from is failure to maintain cleanliness and order. They will spend hours or even days cleaning their homes, only for them to quickly return to a messy state.

This problem can be avoided with only a 10 to 15-minute maintenance clean each day. This can be as simple as putting objects in their proper place, cleaning up trash, and quickly cleaning the floor.

We will handle this problem by giving you a few steps each day that you can perform to keep your house clean and organized, helping you to avoid those long and unnecessary cleaning sessions that everyone hates.

Chapter 2: Overcoming the Problems

Mindset

Naturally, cleaning isn't fun for most people. If you find yourself struggling to get started and falling into the procrastination trap, try getting into an uplifting move. Just like we motivate ourselves with pump-up music to go the gym, the same technique can be applied to cleaning. Blast your favorite music, dance around, drink a coffee, and get your blood flowing. If you're tired and feeling down, you will have a much harder time cleaning. This is why we recommend you start as early as possible when you are refreshed and ready to go. Once those afternoon hours come around, you are likely to crash and put off the rest of the cleaning project until another day.

Practice Cleaning

How many times have you found yourself starting to clean only to get distracted within a few minutes? A simple conversation with your spouse, children needing attention, an old item that brings up memories, or a cell phone call, can make you lose all momentum and progress that you achieved. The best way to combat this issue is with the 25 minutes of pure cleaning technique. The system works like this: You work for 25 minutes without interruption and deal with any problems or issues with a 5-minute break. Studies have shown that 25 minutes is the perfect amount of work our brains can process before we begin to daydream and lose focus. This means that you will be able to achieve 50 minutes of work an hour and have 10 minutes of break time. You may be surprised at how much you can accomplish in 25 minutes because very few of us take the time to actually focus 100% on our work.

Tools

We recommend that after you have invested in the proper tools you invest in one more item: a carrying container. You can buy a professional cleaning carrier or you can purchase a milk carton to carry all your supplies.

Store all your cleaning supplies in milk crates and stack them in a closet. This will help you save valuable storage space under your sinks and cabinets and on your shelves.

If you take the time to organize your milk containers according to the cleaning job for which you use them, you will be able to quickly find the supplies you need. These crates are also very easy to handle and carry around.

Changing Rags

One quick tip we want to sneak into this chapter is to make sure you are frequently changing your rags. Many cleaners will try to use one or two rags and clean their entire house. This not only makes it more difficult to clean, but it can be hazardous to your health. Spreading chemicals or bacteria from one room to another, especially the kitchen, can have terrible consequences. Rags are sometimes difficult to tell if they are dirty and need to be replaced. If you find yourself wondering if your rag needs to be retired, remember this phrase: "When in doubt, throw it out!"

Patience

While it may seem like a good idea to have one big cleaning weekend, we sometimes recommend that you take a different approach. Instead devoting a few days to a bulk clean, try allocating a few hours each day to take care of room at a time. 50 minutes of solid cleaning time, with our 25-minute technique, can put a dent in even the dirtiest room. This Would encourage you to clean the rest of the house. Large cleaning sessions may be necessary but the daunting challenge of cleaning your whole house may be too mentally tough to overcome. So if you find yourself falling into the bad habits we mentioned before, try breaking down your cleaning into smaller more manageable chunks.

Rewards

If you want to reinforce good cleaning habits, we recommend that you create a reward system for yourself. Since you worked so hard to clean or you have been committed to performing maintenance cleaning each day, you deserve a reward for your efforts. Treat yourself to a day at the spa, a special treat, or an item that you have been wanting to purchase. Reinforcing good habits with rewards will strengthen those habits and eventually make them part of your life. You will begin to find yourself thinking about the reward instead of how hard or how miserable cleaning will be. This is the first step of process to keep a clean and organized house for the rest of your life!

Chapter 3: How to minimize Tasks

Moderation is an aptitude that should be produced and sharpened after some time. We exceptionally prescribe you begin gradually and build up your moderate propensities over a timeframe. There is solid proof to demonstrate that individuals who begin rapidly and "cleanse" every one of their assets have high backslide rates once more into consumerism.

The reason is that while we needn't bother with every one of the things we possess; an expansive cleanse can abandon us feeling void. This inclination is just supplanted by buying new things, consequently the backslide. Then again, on the off chance that you begin gradually and make it a need to evacuate things you don't require after some time, your prosperity rate will be much higher!

One Item a Day

If you can train yourself to remove one item that is unnecessary in your home each and every day, you will quickly make a great deal of progress. When evaluating an item, ask yourself what the item's purpose is in your life. Does it bring you any satisfaction? Do you plan to use this item in the future? You then have three options you can choose from: keep it, donate it, or throw it away. Try to remove one item each day until you are struggling to find new items to remove.

Defense

Now that you are actively removing redundant or useless items from your house, you also need to prevent yourself from adding more unwanted items. Many people will take the first step and remove an item a day, but they will also add two useless items each day. The math doesn't add up! So you also need to practice discipline and play some defense. Each time you go shopping, try to remove an item that you don't need from your list or try to find the cheapest option that stills leaves you satisfied. Ask yourself the same questions we mentioned above. One item doesn't seem like a big difference, but that is not the point. The point is to get you actively thinking about your purchasing decisions and really beginning to see the world through the eyes of a minimalist.

Being Smart About Purchases

Just as we want you to remove one item from your house each week, try removing or reducing one purchase from your budget each month. This can mean removing or lowering your cable bill, working on ways to reduce your electricity usage, ending magazine subscriptions, lowering your gas bill, or focusing on lowering food costs. Each month, make it a priority to research and really tackle one finance charge. There are numerous resources and first-hand stories out there of people who have tackled each item and have successfully lowered their bills. You can find these stories and techniques with a simple Google search.

Decisiveness

When it comes to cleaning and removing useless items from your life, you need to make it a priority to be decisive. Remember you have three options: keep it, donate it, or trash it. This may seem easy to most people but many suffer from indecisiveness. The item they are questioning is of no value to them, but instead of trashing it or donating it they begin to wonder if the item really is useless. Their mind begins to wander and the longer they take to make a decision, the more likely they are to keep the useless item. If you don't anticipate using the item in the next three months, then you most likely shouldn't keep it.

Discipline

The most important habit you can grow and develop in both minimalism and in life is discipline. There are numerous surveys that have proven that the IQ of a person and scores in tests don't have a correlation with success in life. Discipline, though, is the main factor that shows a positive correlation with success. We naturally have a tendency to accept short-term benefits while sacrificing our long-term goals. If you can practice discipline and focus long-term at the expense of the short-term, you will live a more fulfilling and successful life. Reward yourself with long-term goals and incentives. Make sure you are aware of when you are practicing discipline and you understand that you are making the right choices.

Reflection

Take time either at the end of each week or the end of each month to reflect on your finances, living situation, and overall satisfaction with life. Your results may be volatile at first as you begin your journey living a life of minimalism, but overall you should begin to see an uptick in all aspects of your life. Reflection allows you to identify your strengths and weaknesses and mentally reward yourself for making the correct decisions. This creates a spiral of success and will really allow you to streamline and improve your progress as a minimalist.

Chapter 4: Minimizing Tasks

We went around and asked a few seasoned minimalists to compare their lives before and after their transformations. Even though we interviewed a few dozen minimalists, they all had similar responses. So let's take a look at the common benefits that most people noticed once they started practicing minimalism.

Focus

The main solution for our study was that having less things to do prompts more concentrate on what makes a difference most in life. Numerous individuals have such a great amount of going ahead in their lives that never give any one assignment all their core interest. They will regularly start to consider the following errand even before finishing the one that is directly before them.

This prompts them surging however an errand and not being completely ready to appreciate it. How often have you experienced difficulty sitting through and appreciating a motion picture since you were pushing about what should have been done when the motion picture was done? This kind of attitude just prompts extra push and can make it extremely troublesome for you to unwind and make the most of your life.

One issue that numerous individuals experience the ill effects of is an interminable negative criticism circle. This means these individuals concentrate on every one of their issues rather than the worth and great things that happen in life. This causes them to concentrate all their time and vitality on negative considerations, which thusly makes more cynicism. Moderation then again helps you concentrate on your life's objectives and your one genuine reason. By centering your time and vitality on what makes you glad, you will see a diminishing in antagonism and an expansion in inspiration.

More Time

When you invest the vast majority of your energy cleaning and sorting out your home, you may think that it's hard to set aside a few minutes for yourself. After work, running errands, and cleaning your home, it is in all likelihood time to at the end of the day go to quaint little inn yourself for one more day. This can turn into a consistent cycle which prompts practically zero downtime for yourself. By embracing a moderate hierarchical style, you will soon wind up with less cleaning to do and more opportunity to spend unwinding.

Less Pressure

Since we were young, the idea of becoming rich and powerful has been drilled into our brains. Our parents always expected straight as and for us to become great doctors or lawyers. While we may not have turned out to be great doctors and lawyers, this pressure to perform and keep making more money is with us day in and day out.

The pressure to keep up with our friends and relatives is usually what causes most of our stress. But many people don't realize that they are already at an income level that will bring them true happiness. By adopting a minimalist lifestyle, they can live the life they want to live without the pressure. You can only make so much before you begin to see diminishing returns, and many people are already beyond that point.

Smarter Purchases

If you follow our guidelines and keep purchases to a minimum, you will find that when you do make a purchase, the item will be one that brings you joy. Instead of having ten pairs of heels, you will only have one or two pairs that you absolutely love. When practicing minimalism, you will find that you will use all the items in your home more frequently - ideally almost daily.

Gone are the days where you would have one dress and use it only twice a year. This will give you more satisfaction and appreciation for all the items in your home. The shift towards minimalism has been growing rapidly over the last few years. Millions of minimalists that have shifted their mindsets are experiencing numerous benefits day in and day out.

A more fulfilled life, more energy, and a general purpose in life are just a few. Before we begin to help you change your life by adopting the minimalist lifestyle, we will quickly talk about a few of the benefits that you will experience with the shift to minimalism.

Stress Reduction

Have you ever noticed that the people that consume the most or have the most objects are usually the most stressed people you know? This isn't a new phenomenon and we have seen it over and over again, especially in the last few years. Those people we envy, who we think have it all, are usually stressed out and very close to a nervous breakdown. You see this all the time with celebrities and constant drug use.

The problem is that these people are replacing a void in their lives by purchasing and consuming. Each new purchase brings them a quick rush of endorphins that quickly fades after a few days. After a while, they lose this endorphin rush and are surrounded with numerous objects that only make them more miserable.

Instead of focusing on keeping up with the Jones's, instead focus on what really makes you happy.

You can change your life by focusing on activities, spending time with loved ones, and following your passion instead of consuming. Adopting a minimalist mindset will allow you to free yourself from the chains of society, and many people fail to see how powerful and liberating this experience can be. Stress in our lives comes from many different sources, but almost all of them are tied to consuming objects in one way. So if you can break the chains of consumerism, you can essentially free yourself from stress.

More Money

One common misconception about people who practice minimalism is that they are poor and can't afford common luxuries. This couldn't be further from the truth. Actually, many minimalists are wealthier then their consumer counterparts.

Many millionaires live in simple homes, drive cars that have good gas mileage, and fill their homes with only the essentials. Minimalism will let you save money and spend it on what matters most to you. So in a sense, minimalists are both financially and spiritually wealthier than their consumer counterparts.

By focusing on what is important in your life and removing everything else, you will also find a great deal more time in your day. All the time you spent worrying or on other activities that brought little to no value is now free to spend on other things. An increase in time is one of the first benefits that new minimalists experience.

Many people underestimate the amount of time we spend researching, browsing, and looking for new purchases, and the amount of time we spend at the mall shopping for items that we will barely use. All this time can be devoted to our one true purpose in life

A Sense of Fulfillment

All of these benefits culminate in one main benefit: a new purpose and fulfillment in life. When you break down your life to just the minimum, it will allow you to see and focus on what matters most to you.

When you shift spending your time on useless activities to spending it on those that bring you true happiness and joy, you will naturally see an increase in life quality.

Minimalism is growing at a rapid pace for a reason, and more people will realize the benefits in the next decade as we, as a society, attempt to shift our mindset from consumption to minimalism.

Chapter 5: Cleaning Your Room

The first area that we are going to organize is your bedroom. Keeping a clean room is essential for health reasons, as this is the room you are going to be sleeping in each night. Failing to clean up food can lead to mold, which you will be breathing in every night if your room is dirty.

Dealing with Clothes

The number one issue of messy bedrooms is poor organization of clothing. When it's the end of the day or we are in a hurry, we tend to leave clothes on the floor. This can ruin clothes and creates an environment that is not organized at all. Make sure you invest in a hamper and make the effort to keep your clothes in the hamper. Sometimes having two hampers, one in the bathroom and one in the bedroom, will remind you to put your clothes away. This makes it a simple trip to the laundry room and you will preserve the long-term life of your clothes.

The Big Picture

Many rooms are cluttered because they are filled with large pieces of furniture. You want to avoid large pieces of furniture in your room unless you absolutely need it. Remember, less is more. Take a good hard look around your room and see if you can move any furniture to another room or if you can remove it completely. Furniture that that doesn't store anything useful or has limited storage capabilities should be replaced with storage-friendly items. You may even think about replacing large, clumsy and awkward dressers and drawers with small, sleek, new dressers and cabinets.

Laundry Hampers

Dirty clothes are the number one reason that your bedroom will appear disorganized and cluttered. Many people will remove clothing and leave it on the bathroom or bedroom floor. This can ruin the clothing as it will be stepped on or, even worse, ripped. If you can take a few extra seconds to properly store dirty clothes, you will improve the life of your clothes and also keep your room organized.

The way to accomplish this is with laundry hampers. Many families usually only have one hamper in their bathroom. This leads to clothes being placed in the proper place when they change to shower or bathe, but when changing occurs in the bedroom, you will be inclined to discard clothes on the floor.

So we recommend a foldable hamper in both your bathroom and bedroom. This way, you are always within a few feet of discarding your dirty clothes. This works great with kids who may become lazy when it comes to discarding dirty clothes in a hamper that is far away.

The Monsters Under Your Bed

The next step is to take a look under your bed. Most people will shove items under their bed such as clothes, trash or luggage. Make sure to get everything out and really ask yourself whether you need it. Under the bed is actually a great storage area.

You can buy large, cheap plastic containers that can hold almost any object and slide them under your bed. This allows you to save space and stay organized at the same time. You can put excess clothes in them or other items that you use only a few times a year that you don't want to get rid of. Store extra sheet sets between your box spring and mattress. This is a great storage tip that will save you space and allow you to easily access the sheets when you want to change your bed.

Making You Own Bed

Want to make your room look clean and organized all the time? Make your bed once you wake up. A bed that is unkempt can make a room look dirty, disorganized, and cluttered. By simply making your bed once you wake up each day, you can improve the look of your room dramatically.

Make it a habit to teach your kids to make their beds before leaving the house. This is a great organizational habit that you can teach them at a young age. Keeping your bed made will also improve the life of your pillows and sheets, as they will not be on the floor getting stepped on throughout the day.

Other Trash

You will want to clean up all trash and debris in your room, particularly any food items. Eating in your room is usually a bad habit, as late night snacks will be left on your bed to stand for days on end.

Empty cups and food containers could grow mold and attract bugs. This is a big problem for any room, but it is magnified because it's your bedroom. You will be breathing in this mold for eight hours a night while sleeping. This could have an adverse effect on your health. A clean room is a must if you want to live a healthy life.

Place small portable trash bins in each room of your house. One reason that most rooms are full of clutter and garbage is because people cannot find the trash can or they are too lazy to walk to the main trashcan in their home.

If you find that your countertops and dressers are full of clutter, try using this tip. These small portable trash cans are also very easy to collect every few days.

Dressers

One of the reasons that rooms become messy in the first place is that people fail to organize their dressers. They have clothes everywhere and when one drawer fills up, clothes will find the floor. Take some time to empty out and clean each of your dresser drawers. Make sure you organize each one, with each drawer responsible for a certain type of clothing. This may take a bit of time but we recommend that if you are going to clean your room, you organize it as well.

Clean and organize one counter or dresser top a day. Remove all the items, clean the dresser or countertop, evaluate which items can be trashed, donated, or kept, and finally return the items. If you can focus on cleaning one dresser or countertop a day, you will quickly remove clutter from your home. Try to be extra strict with items that are on your countertops and dressers as you ideally don't want to have any items on these surfaces.

Declutter Your Room

Try to remove as much clutter from your cabinets, dresser drawers, and night stands as possible. Too many objects will only clutter your room. Keeping your counter tops clean will promote a clean and sleek looking bedroom and will also promote healthy organizational habits.

Keep a hamper in your child's room so they can quickly and easily put all their clothes in the hamper when they change. You may want to move the hamper into the bathroom if you find there are always clothes on your bathroom floor.

Devote 5 Minutes a Day to Keeping a Clean Room. One way to keep your room clean is to devote five minutes to making sure your room stays organized. During these five minutes, we recommend you make your bed, open your windows to let fresh air in, remove any trash, pick up any dirty clothes off the floor, and vacuum your room if you haven't done so in a while. This quick and simple five-minute maintenance will allow you to avoid long, tiresome cleaning sessions that occur when your room becomes very messy.

Vacuuming Your Floor

Finally, you can start the last process of cleaning your room, which is vacuuming the floor. If you have tiled floor and you want to mop, make sure you have swept up any debris or garbage.

Be sure to vacuum your whole floor as allergens and dust will cultivate in hard-to-reach places. You want to make sure you get under your bed as well. Don't be afraid to move furniture around to make sure that you get a really good clean. People will move furniture into their room and it will sit for years without being moved and properly cleaned.

Fresh Air

Now that you have a clean room, open your windows and let in some fresh air. Having a fresh, cool breeze in your room will let it naturally ventilate. Any odd smells or cleaning smells that you have uncovered in the cleaning process will be absorbed by the fresh air.

Conclusion

Thank you again for downloading this book!

Your journey to becoming a minimalist will take months of discipline, hard work, and creativity. But if you stick with the program and really devote yourself to this new lifestyle, you can enjoy the benefits for the entirety of your life.

Here are a few habits that will help you in your journey to become a minimalist:

- If you can reevaluate your transportation habits, you can save money and become healthier at the same time. While commuting to work on a bike is far from ideal, if you look at your schedule you may find a trip to the bank or to the store that can be replaced with a bike ride instead of a car ride.
- The best way to avoid purchasing unwanted items is to avoid unnecessary shopping. Try to only shop when you absolutely need

something. Impulse shopping trips usually end with the purchase of unnecessary items.

- If you can begin to change your mindset, you can change your life. When you see a new product, ask yourself what value that item brings to your life. You will begin to see life in terms of value instead of money. This is the first step to a more fulfilling life.

- There are two types of people: those who want and those who are grateful. Those who want will never have inner peace as they continue to chase their desires. Those who are grateful already have everything they need.

- March to your own beat and avoid the mainstream. If you can identify mainstream brands and trends and avoid them, you will not only save but you will stand out from the crowd.

- The journey to a minimalist life doesn't happen overnight. It will take time and practice to hone your skills.

Keep working hard and good luck!

Finally, if you enjoyed this book, please take the time to share your thoughts and post a review on Amazon. It'd be greatly appreciated!

Thank you and good luck!

Printed in Great Britain
by Amazon

34217945R00030